COLOR & LEARN: WORLD WAR II

A World War 2 History Coloring Book For Everyone!

Color & Learn

If you like the book, please leave a review on wherever you bought
and share your beautiful colored designs with the world.

ISBN-13: 978-1-64845-045-7

GET OUR NEW BOOKS!

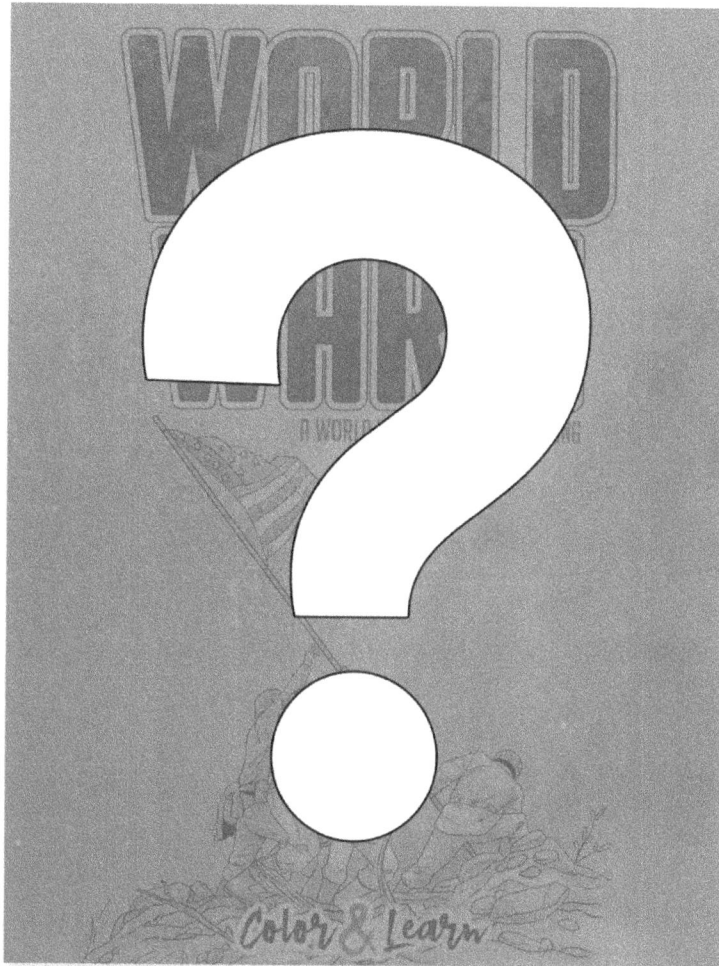

Sign up to our VIP Newsletter to not miss our new book releases
and to take part of **free book giveaways** and so much more!

www.ColorAndLearn.com/free

CONTENTS

INTRODUCTION

World War II was by far the most important war in human history. It lasted from September 1, 1939 to September 2, 1945, and nearly every country in the world was involved in some way. This was a war that was fought on multiple continents, and when the smoke cleared, nearly twenty-five million military personnel had died on both sides and around fifty million civilians had lost their lives. Entire cities were destroyed, populations were displaced, and millions of people were placed in concentration camps. Even the borders of Europe and Asia were redrawn.

During the first two years of the war it looked like Japan would easily conquer Asia, as well as Germany and its allies taking large parts of Europe and North Africa. There seemed to be nothing the people of the world could do, as city after city and then country after country fell to the Axis forces.

The tide of the war began to change in late 1941 and early 1942 in both the Pacific and European theaters of the war. The Soviet Union was able to use a combination of its physical land size, large population, and extreme weather conditions to its advantage, while the entrance of the United States on the Allied side meant that the Axis had to contend with a new, large army that appeared to have unlimited resources.

When World War II finally ended, the borders of Asia and Europe were remodeled, with the Soviet Union and the United States becoming the two dominant superpowers.

Read ahead and learn about this important period in world history and take part by coloring the amazing illustrations showing different aspects of World War II.

WORLD WAR I

It is important to know that as horrific as World War II was, it didn't just happen overnight. There were several big events that led up to it, and most of them were very bad! In the early 1900s, many of the governments of Europe were trying to expand their countries. They usually did this through warfare.

The country of Great Britain became powerful by taking over smaller countries all over the world. France also became powerful by conquering smaller countries.

Smaller countries that are ruled by more powerful countries are known as *colonies.* Colonies often have nice possessions like tea, coffee, and even gold. The more powerful countries like to control them so they can get more of those nice things. The country that rules over the colonies is known as a *mother country* and together they are known as an *empire.*

Russia was another major country in Europe that wanted to expand. To the east of Russia there was a lot of land and not many people, so it expanded in that direction.

The country of Germany was between Russia, Great Britain, and France. Germany wanted more land too, but most of the colonies of the world were already taken by Britain and France. Germany then started thinking of taking land in Europe.

To stop Germany from expanding, Britain, France, and Russia formed an *alliance.* An alliance is when countries make a pact of friendship. Countries in an alliance agree that if one of the friends, or *allies*, is attacked by an outside country, then they will come to its aid. These three countries became known as the *Triple Entente*.

Germany also formed an alliance. Germany made allies with two other countries: Austria-Hungary and the Ottoman Empire. The Ottoman Empire was the country known as Turkey today, along with all the colonies it ruled. These three countries became known as the *Central Powers.* Other countries would later join both alliances.

When the prince of Austria-Hungary was assassinated in 1914, a small country named Serbia was blamed. Austria-Hungary declared war on Serbia, but Russia was Serbia's ally. Soon, all European countries were declaring war on each other.

This turned into **World War I**, which lasted from July 28, 1914 to November 11, 1918.

It was a real mess and millions of people died on both sides before it was over.

Eventually, Germany and its allies lost the war. They had to pay huge amounts of money and give lots of their land to the winners.

Europe 1914

N
S

ICELAND

ATLANTIC OCEAN

NORWAY

SWEDEN

FINLAND

RUSSIA

IRELAND

NORTH SEA

GREAT BRITAIN

GERMANY

FRANCE

AUSTRIA HUNGARY

SERBIA

ADRIATIC SEA

ITALY

PORTUGAL

SPAIN

GREECE

TURKEY

MEDITERRANEAN SEA

KEY   CENTRAL POWERS   ALLIED POWERS

THE VERSAILLES TREATY

Modern wars always end with the signing of a *treaty*. A treaty is an agreement between the warring countries that decides important issues like the future borders of the countries involved. Treaties also often decide how much the losing country should pay.

After World War I, the warring countries met in Paris at a palace called *Versailles*. Versailles was a historical place because it had been the Royal Palace when France had kings and queens. On June 28, 1919, it was the location where Germany signed its official surrender.

Austria-Hungary and the Ottoman Empire had already signed separate peace treaties. Both of those countries were broken up into smaller countries and their monarchies (royal families) were abolished. Since Germany was the largest of the Central Powers and had the largest army, it was punished the most by the victors.

Great Britain and the United States (the Americans entered World War I in 1917 on the side of the British and French) wanted to impose an easy peace on Germany. They thought that an easy peace would cause fewer economic and social problems in Germany and Europe.

But since most of the fighting took place in France, the French weren't very happy and wanted to punish Germany.

Eventually, the French got their way!

Under the Versailles Peace Treaty, Germany was forced to give up 13% of its land and was also forced to pay 132 billion *marks* in *reparations*. A mark is what the Germans called their standard of currency at the time, kind of like the dollar in the United States. Reparations are payments that a country or people must make to another country or people for doing something wrong.

Well, 132 billion of any currency is a lot, right? It was too much for the Germans to pay. The high amount of reparations caused a lot of social and economic problems in Germany. Many Germans were angry that they had to pay so much. The high payments also caused *inflation* problems in the German economy. Inflation is when the prices of goods rise very rapidly.

The inflation from the reparations meant that many Germans had a hard time paying their bills.

The Versailles Peace Treaty was supposed to solve problems created by World War I, but we'll see that it created many more problems.

WHO WERE THE NAZIS?

The 1920s was a tough decade in Germany. In addition to losing a lot of their young men in World War I, Germans encountered the severe inflation that we just discussed. More and more Germans began turning to extreme political parties for answers. One extreme party was the *communists*. The communists believed that free trade and private ownership of land should be eliminated. They had many followers among factory workers.

Another extreme political party was the *National Socialist German Workers' Party*. Yes, that name is a mouthful to say, so most people just began calling them the *Nazis* for short. Most of the Nazi supporters were farmers and middle-class business owners and office workers. Both the Nazis and the communists were against the government and the other political parties, but they had very different answers to Germany's problems. The communists wanted to take over the government and then take control over all privately owned companies and land. The Nazis also wanted to take over the government, but they then wanted to also eliminate their enemies.

The Nazis had many enemies, but at the top of their list were the *Jews*. Jews are members of an ethnic and religious community that follows the religion of Judaism.

The Nazis and communists fought each other on the streets of some of Germany's biggest cities in the 1920s and into the 1930s, but their battles were eventually settled in elections.

In 1932 under the leadership of an Austrian born German named *Adolf Hitler*, the Nazis won more votes than any other German political party. Hitler was a World War I veteran who had fought in the German Army. He was known for his excellent public speaking abilities, which he used to stir up large crowds of supporters.

Once Hitler and the Nazis were in power, they quickly quit making reparation payments, rebuilt their military, and started targeting Jews and other enemies of their government.

But Hitler and the Nazis weren't content with just Germany. They had big plans to take over more land in Europe. Besides his great public speaking skills, Hitler made a lot of promises to the German people that helped him get elected. Those promises included rebuilding Germany's military and uniting German-speaking people throughout Europe. Using Germany as his base he wanted to create a German *Reich*. Reich is the German word for empire. Do you remember reading about empires earlier? Hitler and the Nazis wanted to build what was known as the Third Reich, or the third great German empire.

In order to create this German empire, Hitler and the Nazis would need to invade some countries, which Great Britain, France, and other countries would not allow.

By the late 1930s it was clear that Europe was headed for another world war.

THE JAPANESE EMPIRE

You might think that World War I and even World War II were purely European wars. But as the names of those wars indicate, battles in both wars took place around the world. In World War II, even more battles were fought outside of Europe. Many battles were fought in North Africa, while others were fought in Asia and the Pacific. This was because Japan had embarked on the same idea of conquest as Germany.

In the years after World War I, the idea of *fascism* became popular throughout the world. Fascism was a political idea where only one political party rules the government. Fascists (people who believed in fascism) were also extreme *nationalists*. Nationalists believe that their country is great, while fascists believe that their country is better than others. In the 1930s, the Nazis were fascists and so was the government of Italy. Japan's government also had a lot in common with fascism, so in 1936 the leaders of Japan, Germany, and Italy formed an alliance known as the *Axis Powers*.

Just like in World War I, other countries later joined the Axis Powers, but the three main countries were always Germany, Italy, and Japan. All three countries had plans to expand their borders through military force, but Japan was the first country to do so.

On September 18, 1931, Japan invaded the Chinese province of *Manchuria*. Many historians believe that this was the date of the true start of World War II. The Japanese believed that it was their right to rule over their Asian neighbors. They wanted to build an Asian empire that they called the *Greater East Asia Co-Prosperity Sphere*. It was certainly quite a big name, but after all, Japan was trying to build quite a big empire.

Italy followed Japan by invading Abyssinia (Ethiopia) on October 3, 1935 in order to create its empire.

At this point, most of the world knew it was only a matter of time until war returned to Europe. It had been about twenty years since the end of World War I, but things weren't looking good for lasting peace. The Americans were giving supplies to the Chinese fighting the Japanese, so many believed that a war would start between Japan and the United States. But most people of the world were waiting breathlessly for the first conflicts in Europe to begin.

Unfortunately, they wouldn't have to wait long.

A FINAL CHANCE FOR PEACE

In 1938, many people still hoped that Europe could avoid war. The leaders of Great Britain and France thought that they could bargain with Hitler and the Nazis, and if they were given some more land, they would be happy.

Germany's first step was to incorporate the independent country of Austria into its Reich on March 12, 1938. Most Europeans didn't care though, because Austria was a German speaking country. Film footage shown at the time presented that most Austrians were happy with being under Nazi rule. The Germans called the union with Austria, the *Anschluss*. Anschluss is a German word meaning "joining."

But Hitler and the Nazis weren't done with their bloodless conquests. Hitler next turned his attention to the independent country of Czechoslovakia. Although most of the people in Czechoslovakia were either Czechs or Slovakians, there were also many German speaking residents living in a region of the country called the *Sudetenland*. Hitler told the world that he only wanted the people of Sudetenland to unify with the rest of Germany. To many European leaders it sounded like a reasonable request.

The leaders of Great Britain and France traveled to Munich to meet with Hitler and the Nazi leaders about the political situation. Hitler assured them that once Germany was given the Sudetenland, they would quit expanding their territory. The other leaders of Europe wanted to avoid war so badly that they agreed. On September 30, 1938, the leaders of Great Britain, France, and Italy signed an agreement known as the *Munich Agreement*. The agreement allowed the German army to occupy the Sudetenland.

You're probably wondering what the Czechoslovakia government had to say about the agreement, right? Well, they weren't even included in the talks! Europe's biggest countries decided what was best for Czechoslovakia and there was nothing the smaller country could do about it.

Overall, though, most Europeans were happy with the agreement because it appeared to prevent another war.

But then on March 13, 1939, German troops marched into the rest of Czechoslovakia. The leaders of Britain and France made public statements that their countries were outraged over the situation, but Hitler and the Nazis knew they weren't going to do anything to stop them.

Nazi Germany believed it had a green light to go ahead with its conquests. The other nations of Europe appeared either unwilling or unable to do anything about Germany's aggression. Europe and the world were about to experience another world war; a war that would be much worse than the first one.

FIRST QUIZ TIME!

1. What was the name of the peace treaty that ended World War I?

   a. Heimlich Treaty
   b. Harper's Ferry Treaty
   c. Versailles Treaty

2. Who was the leader of the Nazi Party?

   a. Franklin Roosevelt
   b. Adolf Hitler
   c. Winston Churchill

3. The alliance between Germany, Italy, and Japan was known as the:

   a. Axis Powers
   b. Super Powers
   c. New Alliance

4. The treaty that gave Nazi Germany control over part of Czechoslovakia was:

   a. Munich Agreement
   b. Memphis Agreement
   c. Lunch Agreement

5. The German word for empire is?

   a. Mark
   b. Reich
   c. Ost

INTERESTING QUOTES

The only thing we have to fear is fear itself.
Franklin D. Roosevelt – March 1933

The fruits of victory are tumbling into our mouths too quickly.
Emperor Hirohito of Japan – April 1942

The eyes of the world are upon you. The hopes and prayers of liberty-loving people everywhere march with you.
Dwight D. Eisenhower – June 1944

THE FIRST SHOTS ARE FIRED

Most historians say that World War II officially began when Germany invaded Poland on September 1, 1939. Even after taking over Czechoslovakia and Austria, Hitler still wanted more land, so he turned his eyes to Germany's eastern neighbor, Poland. Remember how Germany lost a lot of its land because of the Versailles Peace Treaty? Well, some of that land Germany lost was given to Poland. Hitler wanted the land back and so he invaded Poland. Great Britain and France could not just stand by, so they declared war on Germany.

But Great Britain and France didn't send any help.

The Polish were left to fight the Germans by themselves and it was a fight they weren't prepared for. On the other hand, the Germans had *mobilized* for war. *Mobilization* is when a country prepares for war, months or even years ahead of time by building tanks, planes, guns, and other equipment. Mobilization is also when a country recruits and trains men for its military.

Poland had a pretty large army before World War II, but it was mainly infantry and many of them still rode horses! On the other hand, the German army was complete with hundreds of tanks, heavy artillery, bomber and fighter planes, and paratroopers (soldiers who parachute from airplanes). The Germans also used a military strategy against Poland called *blitzkrieg*. Blitzkrieg is a German word that means "lightning war." It was named blitzkrieg because it happened so quickly; first the Germans bombed the enemy with planes, then their artillery, then the tanks and infantry were sent in to mop up.

The Polish fought hard, but they just couldn't stand up to the advanced German technology and tactics. To make matters worse, they were invaded on their eastern border on September 17 by the Soviet Union (the Russians). All the fighting in Poland was over by October 6 and the Germans and Russians were able to split what was left of the country between them.

The world was frightened and shocked by how quickly Germany was able to conquer Poland. People were also wondering why France and Great Britain hadn't done anything to help Poland.

WHAT WAS THE SOVIET UNION?

In order to understand World War II better, it is important to understand what the Soviet Union was. To do that, we need to first go back in time a few years to before the start of World War II.

During World War I, Russia had a lot of problems and eventually their king, who they called a *tsar*, was overthrown. The people who overthrew the tsar were communists. The communists established a communist dictatorship in Russia in 1918 and eventually expanded their control over some of Russia's smaller neighboring countries. Ukraine, Lithuania, Latvia, Estonia, and Armenia were just a few of the smaller countries that were brought under the rule of this communist empire in 1922. The communists named their new empire the *Soviet Union*. The word "soviet" is a Russian word for "council" or "advice" and "union," of course, refers to all the smaller countries, or republics, that comprised this new empire.

Communist Russia's first leader was Vladimir Lenin. He worked hard to apply communism rules to the country, but also had to fight a civil war against other groups who didn't want communism. The communists won the civil war in 1922, which is also when a new leader named Joseph Stalin came to power.

Stalin was born with the name Ioseb Bsarionis dze Jughashvili in the small country of Georgia in 1878. He moved to Russia as a young man and changed his name to Stalin, which is Russian for "steel." Stalin ruthlessly worked his way through the communist government until he finally became the leader of Russia. Once Stalin was the leader, he led Russia on a campaign of conquest, creating the Soviet Union.

Any country that opposed Stalin was ruthlessly defeated by the Soviet military or by other means. For example, when the people of Ukraine refused to cooperate with Stalin's ideas, he had their crops taken away, leading to the deaths of millions of Ukrainians.

Stalin justified his ruthlessness by saying that he was doing those acts for the good of the people. Supporters of communism around the world believed what Stalin said, but they were confused when he signed an agreement with Nazi Germany to *partition* Poland. A partition is when a country is broken up into smaller countries by a bigger country or several countries.

The British and the French were the most confused and frightened about the agreement. They thought that Hitler was bad enough, but when Stalin started taking over other countries they became really frightened. Now they had to contend with two dictators commanding two very large armies.

THE INVASION OF THE WEST

After Germany and the Soviet Union invaded Poland, the British and the French did what they could to prepare for war. Because Britain and France were *democracies*, unlike Germany and the Soviet Union, they had to have votes to decide what to do next. A democracy is a government where the people decide their leaders through free elections, and although it is the fairest type of government, debates over what to do can take time. The decision was for the British to send some of their troops to France, while the French waited patiently behind the *Maginot Line*.

The Maginot Line was a collection of fortifications the French built along their border with Germany during the 1930s. The French didn't want to get invaded again by Germany, like they had been in World War I, so they built the Maginot Line to prevent that. The problem was France also had a border with Belgium. Countries don't tend to follow the rules during wars, so instead of trying to cross the French border at the tough Maginot Line, Germany invaded France through the *Low Countries*. The Low Countries are the small countries just north of France: Belgium, the Netherlands, and Luxembourg. They are called the Low Countries because they are at a low elevation next to the Atlantic Ocean.

The Germans surprised the British and the French by avoiding the Maginot Line and invading the Low Countries on May 10, 1940. The Germans used their blitzkrieg strategy to move quickly through the small countries. There were few troops there to stop the Germans and the terrain was easy for their tanks to cross. The Germans had conquered the Low Countries within three weeks and were now ready to invade France through its northern border at the Ardennes Forest.

After facing heavy French resistance south of the Ardennes Forest, the bulk of the German army swept across the plains while another detachment chased the British forces back to the coast.

The British forces in France, known as the *British Expeditionary Forces (BEF)*, began evacuating France at the town of Dunkirk on May 27, 1940. The British forces needed to make it across the short distance of the English Channel, but with German bombs coming down on them, they may as well have been trying to get to the other side of the world! Thanks to the aid of British civilians who used their fishing boats, tugboats, and yachts, the majority of the BEF was able to safely evacuate France by June 4, 1940.

France was not so lucky.

The French surrendered to Adolf Hitler and the Germans on June 22, 1940. Hitler was ecstatic over his accomplishment and took the time to personally accept the French surrender.

DID YOU KNOW?

- Benito Mussolini was the leader of Italy during World War II. Like Hitler, he was a fascist dictator. Mussolini came to power in 1922 and Hitler is said to have modeled his style and methods on him.

- After carving up Poland with Germany, the Soviet Union invaded the tiny northern European country of Finland on November 30, 1939. Although the Finns were severely outnumbered by the Soviets, they were able to fight to what was basically a draw on March 13, 1940.

- Winston Churchill became the Prime Minister (leader) of Great Britain on May 10, 1940, just as Germany invaded the Low Countries.

- The smaller European countries of Hungary, Bulgaria, Finland, and Romania would later join the Axis Powers.

- Although most Americans did not support fascism or communism, they wanted to remain neutral, even after Germany began invading other countries.

- Germany invaded Denmark and Norway, known together as Scandinavia, on April 9, 1940. The invasions of those two countries were complete on June 10, 1940.

BOGGED DOWN IN THE BALKANS

While Germany was conquering country after country in Western Europe, Italy decided to do the same thing in southeastern Europe. Do you remember that like Hitler, Mussolini was a fascist dictator? He had big plans of glory and wanted to recreate the Roman Empire with Italy at its center. The problem was that none of the other countries in southeast Europe wanted to be part of Mussolini's new Roman Empire.

So, Mussolini had to use the Italian Army to force the smaller countries to do what he wanted.

The region the Italians especially wanted to conquer was the *Balkans*. The Balkans is short for the "Balkan Peninsula," which includes a few smaller countries, such as Albania, Yugoslavia, Bulgaria, and Greece. Mussolini decided to take the Balkans in one major offensive by invading Greece on October 28, 1940. Greece is a mountainous country that proved to be difficult for the Italian Army. The terrain was tough, and the Greeks fought fiercely to protect their land. There were also several well-trained British troops in Greece who were resupplied by British military bases on the island of Crete.

After the fighting bogged down in the Balkans, Hitler ordered the German Army to invade Greece on April 6, 1941. Hoping to regain land they lost in World War I, Bulgaria joined Italy and Germany in the campaign.

The fighting was fierce, and the Axis forces seemed to make little headway. In addition to fighting the regular Greek and British army units, the Axis forces faced allied *partisans*. Partisans are fighters or soldiers not in official military units.

In order to keep the British from supplying the Balkans, the Germans finally invaded Crete with an *airborne troop* in May. An airborne troop is one that is parachuted into a battle, often behind the lines of combat. Airborne troops are also sometimes referred to as *paratroopers*.

The combination of Axis manpower, German planes, and the invasion of Crete proved to be too much for the Allies. On June 1,1941, the last of the Greek and British troops surrendered. Partisans in the Balkans continued to fight the Italians and Germans for the entire war, but the conquest and occupation of the Balkans had already been completed.

THE BATTLE OF BRITAIN

After France surrendered, only Britain stood in the way of Germany's conquest of all Western Europe. Luckily for Britain, it is an island nation, so conquering it presented a number of problems for the Germans. As soon as France surrendered to Germany, the Germans began building military bases in northern France and the Low Countries. These would be used when they invaded Britain. Hitler and his top generals got together and came up with a plan to invade Britain. They called it *Operation Sea Lion*. The Germans planned to move their large army across the English Channel in thousands of boats. They would then land on the shores of southern and eastern England.

But before the Germans landed any foot soldiers, they had to soften up Britain's defenses.

In preparation for Operation Sea Lion, Hitler decided to use the *Luftwaffe*, or German air force, in a nonstop bombing campaign of Britain's cities and military installations. The German air attacks on Great Britain began July 10, 1940 and became known as *The Battle of Britain*. The Battle of Britain was exclusively an air battle over the skies of Britain that lasted until October 31, 1940.

Hitler and his generals didn't consider that the Royal Air Force (RAF), Britain's air force, was still intact and had plenty of good pilots and excellent planes that were more than a match for the Germans. The British fought fiercely for their country's skies and it wasn't just the RAF pilots who took part in the fighting. Civilians manned anti-aircraft guns in cities and towns throughout Britain, shooting down German bombers and fighters. By October 1, it was clear that the British were winning the battle. During the invasion the Germans had lost 1,733 aircrafts to either British fighters or anti-aircraft fire. The German force was reduced to just 273 planes. On the other hand, the RAF still had 732 planes patrolling their skies on October 1.

The Germans, however, weren't giving up easily on their plans to invade Britain. They kept attacking Britain from the air but changed their strategy to what is known as the *Blitz*. If you remember from earlier, *blitz* is the German word for lightning. Basically, the October 1940 Blitz involved the Luftwaffe bombing civilian targets throughout Britain, especially London. Although the Luftwaffe killed more than 42,000 British citizens during the Blitz, it failed to break the British people's will to fight.

Germany ended the Blitz on October 31, 1940, giving the British their first victory of World War II.

THE DESERT FOX VERSUS THE DESERT RATS

Mussolini had bold plans to build his new Roman Empire. Besides conquering the Balkans, he also wanted to take over most of North Africa. He began this ambitious plan on September 13, 1940, when Italian forces invaded Egypt from Libya. The Italians thought they would quickly overrun Egypt, but the British who were stationed there put up a stiff fight and began driving the Italians back to Libya.

Mussolini turned to Germany once more for help. Germany responded by sending the *Afrika Korps* to Libya on February 14, 1940. The Afrika Korps was an elite German military force that was trained and equipped specifically for desert fighting. They wore special uniforms that protected them from the heat and sand, which even included shorts! The Afrika Korps was trained in state-of-the-art tank tactics. They could maneuver in the desert where there often weren't any roads and where the sand could destroy the engines of vehicles. The commander of the Afrika Korps was Erwin Rommel, who was also known as the *Desert Fox.*

It was the British who nicknamed Rommel the Desert Fox because his maneuvers were so effective, and he was so elusive. Rommel led the Afrika Korps in victory after victory over the British and reached as far as the city of El Alamein, Egypt. The British held the Axis advance at El Alamein in July 1942 and then pushed the Axis forces back in October of that year. This was mostly due to the efforts of British General Bernard Montgomery and the 7th Armored Division, better known as the *Desert Rats.*

The Desert Rats fought in the British Army throughout World War II, but they made their greatest contribution in North Africa. When it seemed as though nothing could stop Rommel and the Afrika Korps, Montgomery and the Desert Rats showed that they could be just as effective. After the British won the Second Battle of El Alamein on November 11, 1942, Hitler had to withdraw forces from the region to fight in Russia and other parts of North Africa.

The Afrika Korps would continue to fight in North Africa until 1943. They won some important battles in that time, but the Desert Rats were the winners in the end.

OPERATION BARBAROSSA

The Nazis were happy with their conquests in Western Europe, but their real plan was to take land in Eastern Europe and to colonize the area. The problem was that the Soviet Union was in Eastern Europe and they were allies with Germany, right? Well, not exactly. Remember how we discussed that the Nazis were against communism? Well, that didn't change once they came to power. Just because they agreed to divide Poland with the Soviet Union didn't mean they changed their minds about communism. It turns out they were just waiting for the right time to catch Stalin and the Soviets off guard.

On June 22, 1941, the German Army, along with troops from the Axis countries of Italy, Hungary, Romania, and Finland attacked the Soviet Union along an 1,800-mile front in Eastern Europe. The Axis Powers attacked with nearly four million men, almost 4,000 tanks, and more than 5,000 planes. The Germans called the attack *Operation Barbarossa*. It was named after a German emperor from the Middle Ages who was known for being a tough fighter.

The plan was to surprise the Soviets and quickly take their capital city of Moscow, forcing a surrender.

The first few weeks of the operation went according to plan. The Axis forces won battle after battle against the surprised and under equipped Soviets. But things began to take a turn when the Soviet Union's two biggest advantages became revealed: the number of their people and the vastness of their land.

Remember that the Soviet Union was Russia plus several smaller countries it controlled? This became a major advantage for the Soviets when they were invaded by the Axis Powers. The Soviets were able to take men from all parts of the Soviet Union, many of whom were from lands to the east that the Axis Powers couldn't reach. The Axis forces may have won more battles and killed more soldiers, but the Soviets had many more troops and were able to send large numbers to the front.

The Soviet Union was also a lot bigger than the Axis forces realized.

The initial Axis attacks in Ukraine went well and it was easy for them to move across the plains. However, they soon found that it was difficult to resupply their tanks, trucks, and planes with gas. In a way, the Axis forces were a victim of their own success.

Finally, the harsh Russian winter came early, which literally froze the Axis forces at the front. Operation Barbarossa officially ended December 5, 1941. Fighting would continue in the Soviet Union and Eastern Europe for the remainder of the war, but land was only gradually taken and then often lost by the Axis. The battles in Eastern Europe became known as the *Eastern Front*.

DID YOU KNOW?

- The German word for tanks is panzer. The word became so common during World War II that it is still used in some non-German speaking countries to describe tanks.

- The period between the time when Germany and the Soviet Union conquered Poland in 1939 and Germany's invasion of Scandinavia, the Low Countries, and France in 1940 was referred to as the "Phony War" by the British. The British called it the Phony War because they knew it was only a matter of time before they would have to fight the Germans.

- The alliance of Great Britain, the Soviet Union, and later the United States and other countries was known as the Allied Nations or simply the Allies.

- The Soviet Union's army was known as the Red Army. It was called the Red Army because red is the traditional color of communism.

- The official name of the German military was the Wehrmacht.

TEVZEMEI
UN
BRIVIBAI

THE JAPANESE INVASION OF INDOCHINA

After Japan had conquered most of China, they turned their attention south to the French colony of **Indochina**. Today, Indochina is three countries: Vietnam, Cambodia, and Laos. The Japanese saw Indochina as their next step to conquer all of Asia. They planned to use this area to build bases so they could invade more countries in the South Pacific, but the French weren't willing to give Indochina up to the Japanese. However, when the Germans conquered France in 1940, the war situation in Asia changed dramatically.

When the Germans conquered France, they installed a pro-Nazi government that was based in the southern French city of **Vichy**. The Vichy government didn't officially join the Axis Powers, but it did collaborate with them. The Vichy government collaborated with Nazi Germany and when the Japanese invaded northern Indochina on September 22, 1940, it gave them little resistance. The Japanese realized that the few French forces in Indochina weren't going to give them too many problems, so they invaded southern Indochina on July 28, 1941. The Japanese allowed the French officials who were willing to collaborate with them to stay in power. Their main interest now was to build military bases in their newly acquired territory.

The situation worried American President **Franklin Delano Roosevelt**. His government had already placed restrictions on trading with the Axis Powers before Japan's conquest of Indochina, but on August 1, 1941, the United States' government placed an oil **embargo** on Japan. An embargo is when a government imposes restrictions and penalties on other governments or private groups because they see them as a hostile foreign government. Since Japan is an island nation with limited oil, it was hoped that the embargo would limit its ability to conduct a war.

Unfortunately, the embargo only seemed to anger the Japanese.

The world waited breathlessly for the Japanese to make their next move, but they remained quiet for nearly three months.

The Japanese had been planning for a war with the United States for several months and everything was going according to their plans. Defeating China was their main priority and also achieving rule over Indochina. But the Japanese knew that the Americans would never let them have the Asian Empire they desired, so on November 26, 1940, a fleet of 33 ships left Japan for Hawaii.

The Japanese weren't going to let the American make their own decisions, they were going to force them to enter World War II!

GARAGE

A DAY THAT WILL LIVE IN INFAMY

On the morning of Sunday, December 7, 1941, when most Americans were either sleeping or getting ready to go to church, the Japanese fleet attacked Pearl Harbor, Hawaii. Hawaii wasn't yet an American state, but it was a territory and the home of many American military bases. In fact, Hawaii was home to the United States' entire Pacific Fleet, which is what the Japanese intended to wipe out on that fateful morning.

The Japanese attack was swift and destructive. More than 300 Japanese planes launched from aircraft carriers, attacking Pearl Harbor in two waves. The Japanese bombers were protected *Zeros*. The Zero was the name of the best and most deadly Japanese fighter plane. The Zeros protected bombers from American fighters and *strafed* ships and people on the ground. *Strafing* is a military technique where fighter planes attack people and objects on the ground with their machine guns.

The Japanese also used submarines to attack the harbor. Although submarines had been used in World War I, they were still fairly new and could often avoid detection.

Both civilians and military personnel in Hawaii heroically tried to help put out fires caused by the bombing and many anti-craft guns, but the organized quick strike by the Japanese was devastating. The attack on Pearl Harbor killed 2,325 Americans, damaged 21 American ships and destroyed 3. The most famous ship that was sunk in the attack was the Arizona, which has a well-known memorial that you can visit today.

The attack was over nearly as quick as it began. It had begun at 7:55 in the morning and was over at 9:45, lasting just under two hours.

After the attack the United States declared war on Japan. As a result of this, Japan's allies, Germany and Italy, then declared war on the United States. America was officially in World War II. The Japanese had hoped to destroy the American Pacific Fleet with the surprise attack on Pearl Harbor, but it had also angered the Americans who now tried to persuade those who favored *neutrality* to support the war effort. Neutrality means when countries don't support either side. The day after the attack, President Franklin Roosevelt gave a famous speech to an emergency session of Congress. Although the speech only lasted seven minutes, Roosevelt calmed and rallied the American people. He stated that December 7, 1941 was a *"date which will live in infamy."*

The Pearl Harbor attack led many American men to volunteer for the military and inspired women to do what they could by volunteering and working in factories.

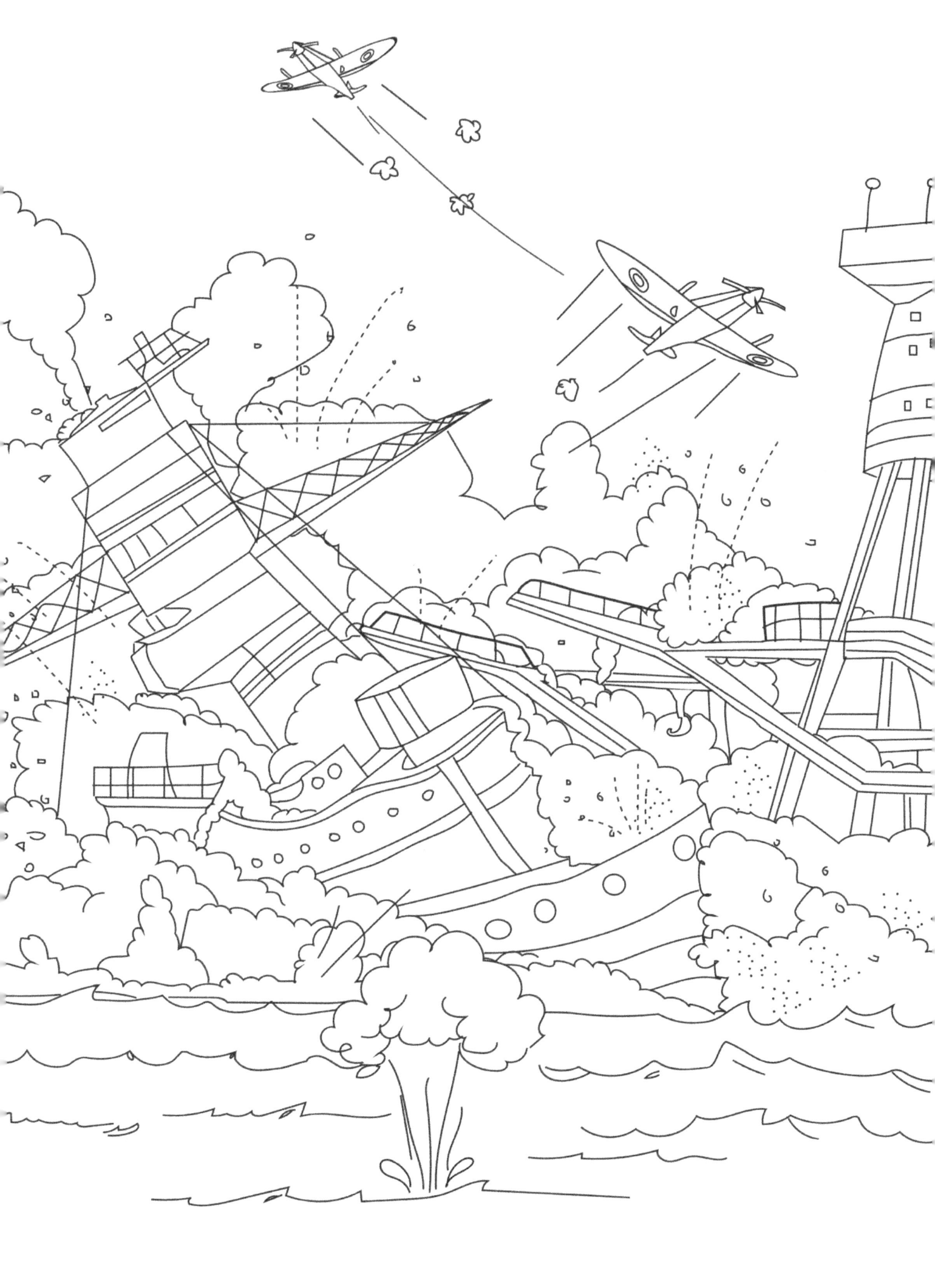

"I SHALL RETURN"

The attack on Pearl Harbor was part of a much bigger plan that the Japanese had to drive all the Allied forces out of Asia. While part of the Japanese Navy was attacking Hawaii, 30,000 Japanese Army troops, supported by fifty airplanes and several ships, attacked the British colony of **Hong Kong**. Hong Kong is a city-state connected to China that became part of the British Empire in the 1800s. Although the British troops in Hong Kong put up stiff resistance to the attack, the Japanese had conquered the colony by Christmas Day 1941.

Just hours after the Pearl Harbor attack, the Japanese also invaded the island country of the **Philippines**. The Philippines is an *archipelago*, or island chain country, located in the south Pacific. The United States took the Philippines from the Spanish in the 1898 Spanish-American War, and after that time they built many military bases on the islands. Much of the American naval fleet that wasn't in Hawaii at the time was in the Philippines, so the Japanese were hoping to destroy all American ships in the Pacific when they invaded the Philippines on December 8, 1941.

The Americans and **Filipinos** (native inhabitants of the Philippines) valiantly fought the Japanese invasion but were ill-prepared. Since the Philippines is close to Japan, the Japanese could easily send reinforcements to the battle.

So, the Americans decided that it was best to retreat with what was left of their fleet intact and fight the Japanese another day. As the Americans were leaving the Philippines, American General **Douglas MacArthur** famously uttered the words, "I shall return." At the time, many people in the world didn't think that it was possible for the Americans to return to the Philippines. The situation in Europe and Asia looked hopeless, with the Axis Powers winning battle after battle. Things looked even worse in the Philippines in the spring of 1942 when the final pockets of American resistance were destroyed.

With the Philippines under Japanese control, the Japanese were able to attack just about any country in the Pacific, including Australia and the United States. But as hopeless as the situation may have looked to many, the entrance of the United States into the war marked the beginning of the end for the Axis Powers. The manpower and industrial might of America proved to be just too much for the Axis forces.

And General MacArthur would keep his promise by returning to the Philippines in 1944.

I SHALL RETURN

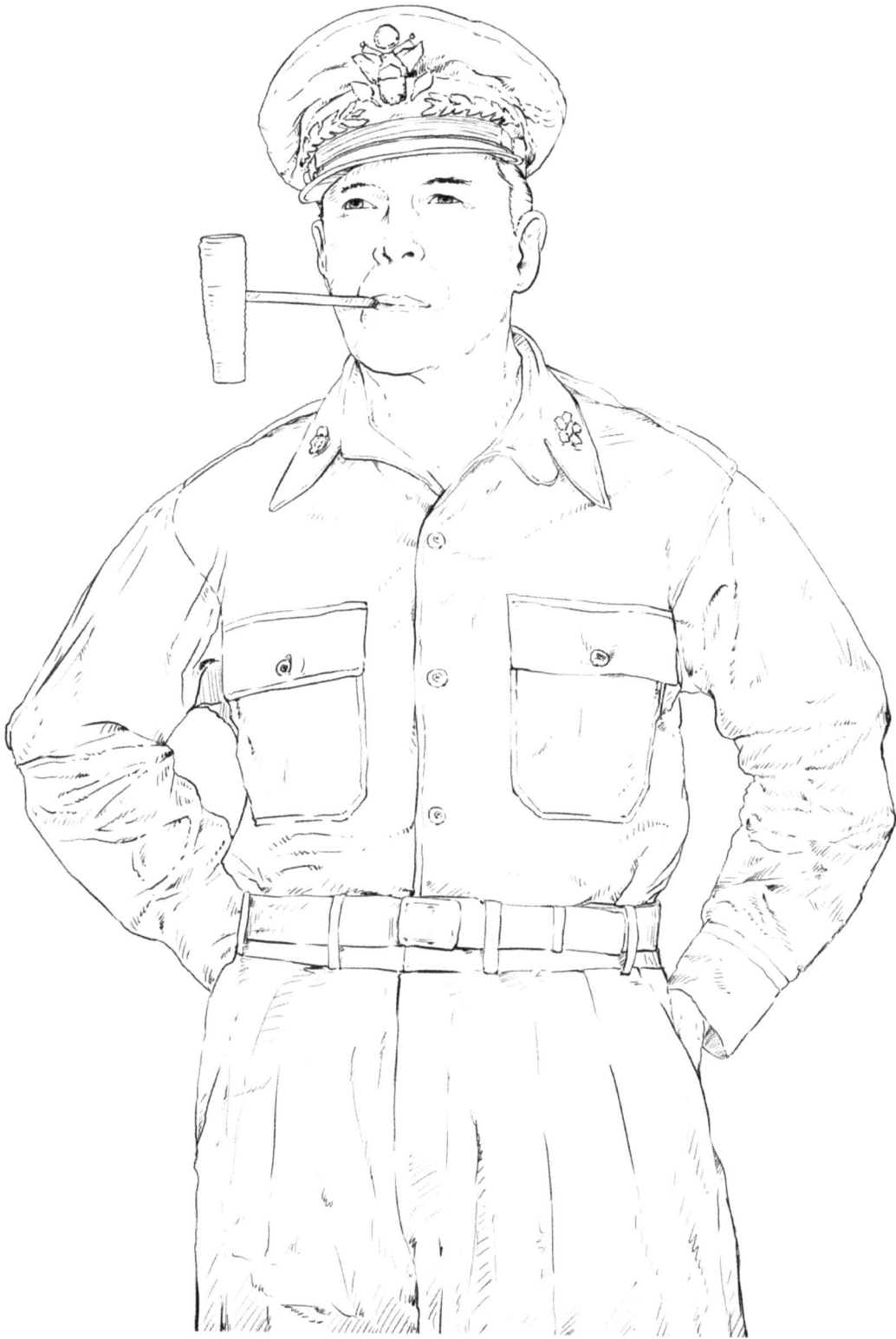

General Douglas MacArthur

SECOND QUIZ TIME!

1. What country did Germany invade to start World War II?

2. What was the date of the Pearl Harbor attack?

3. Where did the Axis Powers attack on June 22, 1941?

4. How did the Germans avoid the Maginot Line?

5. The region of Europe where Bulgaria, Albania, Yugoslavia, and part of Greece is known as?

6. Name one of the Axis Powers besides German:

INTERESTING QUOTES

Never in the field of human conflict, has so much, been owed by so many, to so few!

Winston Churchill – September 1940

Before we're through with them, the Japanese language will be spoken only in hell!

Admiral Halsey – December 1941

Soldiers of the Reich! This day you are to take part in an offensive of such importance that the whole future of the war may depend on its outcome.

Adolf Hitler – July 1943

GERMANY'S SEA WAR

The Germans began World War II with a distinct advantage on land. Because they had mobilized before 1939, they were able to use the element of surprise against other European nations. The Luftwaffe was also a state-of-the-art military organization that proved to be another advantage. But if there was one place where the German military was lacking, it was its navy, known in German as the *Kriegsmarine*.

When World War II began, the British and French had twenty-two battleships and eighty-three cruisers between them, versus only three German "pocket" battleships. Britain in particular had a big head start on the Kriegsmarine. The British had a long history of naval supremacy; it was their navy that had helped them build such a vast empire. The Germans decided to build a massive battleship, which they named the *Bismarck*, after nineteenth century German leader Otto von Bismarck. Disaster struck, however, when the massive ship sank on its maiden voyage in May 1941.

So, the German high command decided to go on another course with its navy.

Since there was really no way that the Germans could catch up to the British Navy in terms of battleships and aircraft carriers, the Kriegsmarine instead built a fleet of deadly submarines known as *U-boats*.

German U-boats attacked Allied naval and merchant ships. They often hunted the waters of the north Atlantic Ocean in groups known as *Wolfpacks,* using radio to communicate with each other. German U-boats were quite effective in the early years of the war, sinking 1,000 Allied ships in 1940 and 1,299 in 1941. This action reduced British exports to almost one-third of its pre-war total. The U-boat fleet peaked in 1942 with around 300 operational, sinking more than 2.6 million tons of Allied shipping materials that year. U-boats were not afraid to go anywhere, sinking merchant ships up and down the east coast of the United States and as far south as South America!

But by the middle of 1943, as the tide began to turn in the European Theater, Hitler decided to allocate more resources to the land forces. Fewer and fewer U-boats were made, which was probably good news for German sailors. Of the 39,000 German submariners (sailors on U-boats) who served in the Kriegsmarine, only about 11,000 survived the war.

THE BATTLE OF MIDWAY

After the United States officially entered the war, President Roosevelt met with the leaders of the other Allied nations to form a plan. It was agreed that most of the group's attention would be given to defeating the Germans and other Axis Powers in Europe. It was argued that Germany posed more of an immediate threat, so American soldiers began going to England to prepare for the eventual Allied invasion of Europe.

Japan, however, was still posing a real threat in the Pacific that couldn't be ignored.

In early 1942, the Japanese still had the capabilities to strike the west coast of the United States. Even if they didn't, they showed no signs of ending their aggression in Asia. But the war in the Pacific *Theater* of operations would be much different than the European Theater. In war terminology, a theater is a location where a few different battles take place. The Pacific Theater of World War II featured many sea and air battles, as opposed to the primarily land battles in the European Theater. Also, the Marines played the major role in American land operations in the Pacific, while the Army was the primary American land force in Europe.

The situation in the Pacific seemed bleak for many years, but the Americans got the victory they needed in June 1942. From June 4 through June 7 of that year, what was left of the American Pacific Fleet fought a Japanese fleet off the tiny American controlled island of Midway. The Japanese hoped to draw what was left of the American fleet out into the open ocean, but they made the mistake of not sending enough ships. The Japanese believed that they had sunk more American ships that they had during the Pearl Harbor attack. The result was that when the Battle of Midway began, the opposing fleets were of nearly equal size.

The Battle of Midway was epic! Planes shot each other down over the ocean and the massive ships fired round after round from their cannons.

When the smoke finally cleared, the Americans had won a clear victory! The Americans had shot down 248 Japanese planes and killed more than 3,000 Japanese sailors and pilots. More importantly, four Japanese aircraft carriers were sunk. Since aircraft carriers were so massive, they took many months to build and were therefore difficult to replace. The Japanese success in the Pacific was dependent on aircraft carriers because that is how they launched many of their aerial attacks. The Pearl Harbor attack was launched from aircraft carriers.

The Japanese forces were on the defensive after the Battle of Midway for the remainder of the war.

AUSTRALIA'S FIGHT IN THE PACIFIC THEATER

The United States Marines and Navy may have done most of the fighting for the Allies in the Pacific, but Australia did more than their fair share for the cause. Australia was located a lot closer to Japan than most of the Allies and as the Japanese moved their way through Southeast Asia, taking country by country, the sparsely populated nation of Australia became a major target.

War arrived in Australia in February 1942, when the Japanese completed a sneak air attack on Darwin. Darwin is a major city in Australia's Northern Territory and at the time had a significant presence of air force and navy bases. The Japanese knew that the Australians could give them some major problems and they wanted to stop the allies using Darwin as a base. The raid began in the morning and consisted of two waves of attacks. The Japanese managed to take out an Australian destroyer, several smaller ships, many planes, and killed more than 230 people. In many ways, the bombing of Darwin was similar to the attack on Pearl Harbor. The attack began in the morning and was launched from aircraft carriers with the intent of taking out Australia's navy capabilities. It was technically a Japanese victory, but it only served to unify Australians and resolve their will to defeat Japan.

The Australians mobilized, and along with the Papuan land forces went on the offensive against Japan in the *Kokoda Trail Campaign,* lasting from July 21 to November 16, 1942. The campaign was named for the Kokoda Trail, a sixty-mile track/trail that connected the town of Kokoda, Papua New Guinea with Port Moresby on the southern coast of the island. Papua was an Australian territory, but on July 21, Japanese forces landed on the north shore of the island and quickly took Kokoda, which had an important airbase.

The Japanese force of about 14,000 men then worked their way south on the trail toward Port Moresby. An Australian force of about 30,000 men began working their way north from Port Moresby. When the two armies met there was heavy fighting and a series of hard-fought battles that took place along the trail. It left more than 600 Australians dead and more than 2,000 Japanese killed. Both sides also had to deal with tough jungle terrain and diseases that were not common to either people. Malaria and dysentery left many on both sides sick and unable to fight.

Eventually, though, the Australians kept fighting, and with the support of native Papuans and some American units were able to drive the Japanese from the island. The Japanese never directly threatened Australia again, and thanks to the American victory at Guadalcanal, the Japanese were now on the retreat in Southeast Asia.

THE BATTLE OF STALINGRAD

When Operation Barbarossa failed, Hitler and his top generals had to come up with a new plan to defeat the Soviet Union. Although the Axis forces had reached the outer suburbs of Moscow, the fighting was extremely costly. The Axis forces were divided primarily into three groups, with the center group pushing towards Moscow. Hitler and the German high command decided that some troops would continue to push onwards to Moscow, but most of their troops would move toward the southern Russian city of *Stalingrad* (now known as Volgograd) on the Volga River. Although Moscow was the capital of the Soviet Union, the Axis commanders believed that Stalingrad was more important strategically.

Stalingrad was a major industrial city and it was also near the major agricultural region of Russia. Perhaps most importantly, Stalingrad's location on the Volga River gave it access to the oil fields of the Caucasus region to the south. Due to all of those reasons, the Axis forces began a major push to take Stalingrad on August 23, 1942.

When the Battle of Stalingrad began, the Axis forces outnumbered the Soviet forces. The Axis had more than 250,000 men, hundreds of tanks, and hundreds of planes. The Soviets had just under 200,000 men and hundreds of tanks and planes.

The fighting was tough and brutal. The Axis forces surrounded much of the city and bombed it around the clock with their planes and artillery, but the Red Army forces just wouldn't leave. The Red Army was resupplied from the Volga River and before long the battle turned into brutal house to house fighting. *Snipers*, (well-trained marksmen), were used by both sides to kill enemy officers.

Finally, on February 2, 1943, the Axis forces retreated from what was left of Stalingrad. The *casualty count* (those killed, wounded, captured, or missing during the battle) on both sides was extremely high. The Axis forces suffered more than 800,000 casualties while the Soviets had more than one million!

Although the Soviets lost more people, the losses proved to be too much for the Axis forces. The Battle of Stalingrad all but wiped out the Romanian, Hungarian, and Italian armies and decimated entire divisions of the Wehrmacht.

The Battle of Stalingrad proved not only to be the most destructive battle in human history, but also the beginning of the end for the Axis forces in Europe. After Stalingrad, Germany, and what was left of its allies, were fighting a defensive war.

THE SIEGE OF LENINGRAD

The Battle of Stalingrad may have been the most destructive battle in World War II, but the Siege of Leningrad went for longer and was maybe just as important. Leningrad (it is now named St. Petersburg as it was before 1918) was just as important to the Soviet Union, strategically and politically. Leningrad was the second largest city in the Soviet Union, was historically the capital city before Moscow, and was home to the Soviet Union's Baltic Sea port. If the Axis forces could take Leningrad it would open the northern thrust of Operation Barbarossa, Army Group North, allowing it to move south to Moscow.

When Operation Barbarossa began, German troops cut off all routes to the south and west of the city while the Finnish army, led by Field Marshal *Carl Mannerheim*, cut off all routes to the north. The people of Leningrad could only be supplied from the east across Lake Ladoga.

The siege of Leningrad officially began on September 8, 1941.

General *Gregory Zhukov* of the Red Army knew that holding Leningrad was just as important as keeping Stalingrad. Neither of those cities could fall to the Axis. The Soviet supply routes ran around the clock across Lake Ladoga and all year-round. During the winter, the Soviets would drive across the frozen lake and in the spring, summer, and fall, they would use boats.

Even so, the Soviets lost many soldiers, civilians, and supplies. The Germans barraged the city nonstop with artillery shelling and aerial bombardments. The Russians did whatever they could to survive the siege, which incredibly went on for more than 900 days!

After the Axis forces lost at Stalingrad and went on the defensive, they moved some of their forces from Leningrad to central Russia. The move allowed the Red Army to lift the siege of Leningrad on January 27, 1944.

To the Red Army soldiers who were familiar with the city, it looked nothing like it did before the war. Nearly every building was damaged, with many completely destroyed, and bodies were strewn all over the streets. The Soviets suffered more than three million military casualties and more than half of Leningrad's civilian population of 650,000 was lost, although most were evacuated. The situation was dire, with civilians even resorting to cannibalism toward the end of the siege.

The Axis forces suffered nearly 600,000 casualties, which effectively destroyed Army Group North.

WOMEN IN WORLD WAR II

There's a lot more to fighting a war than just the soldiers fighting at the front lines. Many more people than the men fighting at the front are needed in support roles, to cook meals, make sure supplies get to the front, and to keep things running properly back home. These non-combat jobs are often called *support roles* or *support units*. Both the Axis and the Allies had plenty of support units during World War II and women often played a major role in them.

Since women were, for the most part, prohibited from combat roles, they served their countries in other ways that were just as meaningful. In the United States, women provided most of the labor in the factories that built weapons for the Allied forces. These included guns, tanks, and planes. For many of these women, it was the first time they had worked outside of the home and earned a paycheck. Their contributions to the war effort were so valuable that the American government created posters and other advertisements to promote women working in arms factories. The most famous of these posters was of a woman nicknamed "Rosie the Riveter." The poster shows Rosie wearing her work clothes and showing her muscles, saying "We Can Do It!"

American women also served in the military in what was known as the Women's Army Auxiliary Corps (WAAC). The women in the WAAC worked mostly as secretaries and nurses but received military benefits and rank.

The situation was similar in the Soviet Union with women filling the factories to make armaments. But because most of the fighting on the Eastern Front took place in the Soviet Union, women were sometimes forced to fight.

A Russian woman named Lydia Litvyak flew fighter planes for the Red Army and was the first woman to shoot down an enemy plane during World War II. Lydia became famous for her missions and was known as "the White Rose of Stalingrad." After several successful missions, Lydia was shot down over the city of Kursk and died on August 1, 1943.

One of the sober realities of World War II was that the Axis Powers often used concentration camp prisoners to work in their armament factories.

Women and children on both sides of the war often had to deal with harsh conditions and were often forced to hide when the opposing armies marched through their communities. Overall, World War II changed women around the world by making them more independent.

DID YOU KNOW?

- Japan was technically ruled by an emperor during World War II. An emperor is like a king, but in Japan during World War II the military had most of the government power.

- Hideki Tojo was the prime minister and true leader of Japan from October 17, 1941 to July 22, 1944. After the war, Tojo was executed for war crimes on December 23, 1948.

- "Axis Sally" was the name of two different American women, Mildred Gillars and Rita Zucca, who broadcast pro-Axis radio messages to American troops during war. Both women were sent to prison for collaboration.

- "Tokyo Rose" was the name given to several different Japanese women who broadcast pro-Axis English language radio messages to American troops during the war.

- The "grad" in Leningrad and Stalingrad means city, like "ville" or "burg" in America.

- The admiral of the Kriegsmarine during World War II was Karl Dönitz.

OPERATION TORCH

Although the Americans were fighting back against the Japanese in the Pacific, they were also sending most of their men to England to help the British in the fight against the Axis Powers in Europe. The American forces gathered and trained for months while the Allied commanders debated the best policy to invade Europe.

American General *Dwight D. Eisenhower*, who would become president years after the war, was given command of an Allied invasion of North Africa. The Allies gave the invasion the codename *Operation Torch*. Remember that the German Afrika Korps were fighting the British Desert Rats in Egypt and Libya? Well, the Allies planned to attack the Axis forces on the other side of North Africa in the countries of Morocco and Algeria. They then planned to move toward each other, meeting in the middle and surrounding the Axis armies in what is known as a *pincer movement*.

Eisenhower's plan called for transporting more than 100,000 British and American forces on ships from England to three different beaches in North Africa. It was a risky plan, but on November 8, 1942 the invasion began.

Most of the Axis forces defending the beaches in Morocco and Algeria were Vichy French. If you remember, the Vichy French leaders were collaborators with the Axis, but most of the regular soldiers in the Vichy army didn't want anything to do with the Nazis. Although some of Vichy units fought, many of them surrendered. Many of the French wanted to join the Allies and others just wanted to return home to France.

On November 16, 1942 Operation Torch was successfully completed.

Operation Torch proved to be a major Allied victory for many reasons. First, it established Eisenhower as an excellent general. He was later promoted to *Supreme Commander* of all Allied forces in the European Theater of war.

Second, Operation Torch pretty much took the Vichy government out of World War II.

Finally, most of the German and Italian troops who remained in North Africa had to fall back to Italy after losing Operation Torch. The Axis forces were in a defensive struggle from that point on with fighting taking place on multiple fronts.

THE SOFT UNDERBELLY OF EUROPE

Operation Torch ran the Axis forces out of North Africa, but its true purpose was to prepare the Western Allied forces with an invasion of Europe. The British and Americans knew that the Soviets couldn't hold out forever on the Eastern Front, so they began thinking of ways to invade Western Europe to open a Western Front. Stalin feared that the Red Army would run out of men or the will to fight if the other Allies didn't invade Europe quickly, so he kept pressure on them to plan an invasion.

Great Britain's Prime Minister, Sir Winston Churchill, responded to Stalin's repeated requests with an analogy. He compared Europe to a crocodile and said that while hitting its snout would only anger it and make things worse, its underbelly was soft and weak. The Allies therefore decided to first invade Europe's soft underbelly, which they believed was Italy.

After taking North Africa, the Allies staged a major invasion of the Italian island of *Sicily* beginning on July 9, 1943. The Allied invasion of Sicily was codenamed *Operation Husky*.

The Germans and Italians put up fierce resistance during Operation Husky, but the Allies' overwhelming numbers were enough to win the battle on August 17, 1943. The Allies could then use Sicily as a base to invade the Italian mainland and open a second front in the European Theater.

But the Allied victory in Sicily had other positive consequences.

The Italian people were always divided on their support of Mussolini and fascism, and even those who were undecided on the issue didn't really want to fight in what they saw as Germany's war. Mussolini's government collapsed and the dictator then fled to northern Italy to carry on the fight against the Allies. Most of the Italians surrendered at that point and went home or joined the Allies, which meant that the Germans had to do almost all the fighting in Italy.

The Germans created heavy fortifications that stretched across the entire Italian Peninsula. The fortifications included ditches, barbed wire, and landmines, which took away some of the numerical advantage that the Allies had.

So, the Allies decided to go around the fortifications!

On January 22, 1944, British and American forces began landing on the beaches near the city of Anzio in a major *amphibious assault*. An amphibious assault is when a military force launches an attack from the sea to the land. After losing thousands of men and fighting for several months, the Allies were finally able to take Anzio on June 5, 1944. The Italians were out of the war and Mussolini was executed by his own people less than a year later.

ISLAND HOPPING

As we discussed earlier, the European Theater and Pacific Theater of World War II were totally different for several reasons. First, the Pacific Theater mainly involved the Americans fighting the Japanese, while the European Theater saw more countries involved in the fighting. Second, the European Theater was primarily fought on land, while in the Pacific fighting was often on small islands only a few miles wide.

If you look at a map, Japan is a long way from the United States, thousands of miles across the Pacific Ocean. Getting a military force from the United States to Japan via the ocean was no easy task. The Americans couldn't just bring the entire force across the ocean all at once. There just wasn't enough fuel and other resources to do that and the Japanese also had easily attacked the American forces if they were all in one group.

The Japanese had occupied several small islands in the Pacific. So, the American high command knew that they would need to capture some of those islands along the way to Japan, but they just didn't have the manpower to take them all. The Japanese were tough fighters and often fought to the last man. So, the Allies decided that they would only invade certain islands and *leapfrog,* or *island hop* those that were deemed less important.

The Americans long-term island-hopping strategy began on August 7, 1942 when they invaded an archipelago in the South Pacific known as the Solomon Islands. The battle for the Solomon Islands became known as the *Battle of Guadalcanal,* after the largest island in the chain. The Americans knew that Guadalcanal was an island that couldn't be hopped, because the Japanese had built airstrips there that gave bomber planes the capability of hitting the Allied countries of Australia and New Zealand.

The United States Marines did most of the fighting on land at Guadalcanal. Besides encountering stiff resistance from the Japanese, the Americans also had to deal with hot, humid weather, heavy rain, insects, and poisonous snakes. Guadalcanal was truly one of the worst places any American could find himself during the war.

But the Americans kept on fighting through the harsh elements and strong Japanese resistance. Eventually they began to defeat the Japanese, forcing them to evacuate the islands in January 1943. The Japanese evacuation was complete by February 9, 1943, giving the Americans their first major land victory in the Pacific Theater.

The American high command now had to decide the next island to hop.

THE KAMIKAZES

As the Japanese began losing battle after battle in the Pacific, they faced serious *logistical* problems. Logistics relates to how materials and people are obtained and moved from one place to another. Since Japan is an island nation, it had limited materials to begin with and once they started losing territory to the Americans, they also lost important materials needed to make more weapons and munitions.

The Japanese were also losing thousands of men in every battle.

So, when the Americans began to creep closer and closer to Japan, taking island after island in the Pacific, the Japanese high command decided to use a bold new strategy—the *kamikaze*.

Kamikaze is a Japanese word meaning "divine wind" because the kamikazes were fighter pilots who flew their planes on suicide missions. It may be hard to believe, but kamikazes actually volunteered for their missions! They considered it an honor to give their lives for their emperor and country in such a way. Before flying on their final missions, kamikaze pilots were given a big meal by their commanding officers and thanked for their service in a *Shinto* ritual. Shinto is the native religion of Japan.

Kamikaze pilots would usually fly low to a sea battle and then aim their planes for high value targets, such as aircraft carriers and battleships.

The first kamikaze attacks happened during the Battle of Leyte Gulf (October 23-26, 1944) and continued until the end of the war. It is hard to say for sure how effective kamikaze attacks were, although it is estimated that around 19% of all kamikaze attacks hit their targets, sinking up to fifty American ships and killing approximately 5,000 sailors. The real effect the kamikaze attacks had on the enemy was a psychological one. American sailors never knew when a Japanese Zero was trying to strafe a ship or if it was coming in for a kamikaze attack.

There was no real way for the Americans to protect against or prevent kamikaze attacks.

The Japanese also used a similar strategy on land late in the war. When it appeared that the American Marines were about to take an island or strategic position, the Japanese would sometimes attack in a human wave that usually ended in death for the attackers. The attack was known as a *banzai attack* because banzai means "long life" or "10,000 years" in Japanese. The Japanese believed that dying in a banzai attack was honorable and would give them eternal life after death.

ROCKETS OF DEATH

One of the more interesting aspects of World War II was Germany's development of rocket technology. One of the advantages that the Germans had at the beginning of the war, yet didn't take advantage of until later, was their technology. German scientists developed jet airplanes and rockets before and in the early stages of the war, but most government spending went into the traditional land army.

When Germany started losing, it decided to start using some of these "secret weapons."

Beginning in 1944, the Germans began using the *Vergeltungswaffe* or "vengeance weapons" on the Allies. There were two classes of these rockets: *V-1* and *V-2*. These rockets were launched from German held territory in the Netherlands and England, and later France after the D-Day Invasion. They were aimed at military and civilian targets.

The V-1 rocket was a technological step forward, but the V-2 was even more so. The V-2 rocket was designed by Werner von Braun to be remotely guided and could enter space before returning to hit its target. The Germans began using V-2s against the Allies in June 1944, just as the Allies were landing in Normandy. The V-1 and V-2 rockets killed over 9,000 civilians and did a lot of damage to Allied cities, but it was all too little too late for the Germans.

Allied commanders were amazed when they found the rocket launch sites and where they were constructed in eastern Germany. Although the Allies, especially the Soviets, had experimented with rocket technology before the war, the Germans were far ahead of anything they had done.

After the war, the Americans and Soviets raced to capture as many of the German rocket scientists as possible. Braun and other V-2 rocket scientists went on to help create NASA in the United States, while the Soviets captured their fair share of German scientists and equipment to help create their space program.

THE BURMA CAMPAIGN

If you remember earlier facts in this book, when World War II began Great Britain was an empire with many colonies. Britain's most important colony was India, so when the Japanese began expanding their territory in Southeast Asia, India was also threatened. Beginning in January 1942 and lasting until July 1945, the Japanese made several efforts to advance into India but were stopped in the neighboring country of Burma, which is how this long military campaign got its name.

The *Burma Campaign* was where most British soldiers in the Pacific Theater fought, although most of the allies fighting in the campaign were native Asians. Thousands of Chinese, Indians, and Burmese fought alongside British and American soldiers to stop the Japanese and their Thai allies from taking the region. In the end, the casualty count was very high. There were more than 200,000 casualties on both sides, with many of those the result of jungle diseases.

The Allies eventually won the Burma Campaign, but it was not because the Japanese didn't put up a tough fight or try some interesting things. One of the more interesting acts of the Japanese was to construct a 258-mile railway from Ban Pong, Thailand to Thanbyuzayat, Burma, often referred to as the *Thai-Burma Railway*. Construction on the railway began in June 1942 and was completed in October 1943. The railway went through dense jungles, around mountains, and over gorges and rivers. If it was not for the human toll that was required for its construction, it would be a modern marvel.

The human toll, however, was incredible and the Thai-Burma Railway is today remembered as one of the most central aspects of the war in the Pacific.

The Japanese forced over 200,000 local civilians and about 60,000 Allied prisoners of war to work on the railway. The hours were long, and the job was extremely dangerous, and if the Japanese thought workers weren't working fast enough, they would beat or even kill them. Workers were fed very little, which led many to die of starvation. If workers contracted one of the many jungle diseases or were injured while they worked, they were rarely treated or helped.

It is estimated that around 90,000 civilians and 12,000 Allied POWs died building the Thai-Burma railway.

When the war was over, thirty-two Japanese officers associated with building the Thai-Burma railway were sentenced to death for war crimes.

The railway has been modernized and is still in use today.

D-DAY

Meanwhile in Eastern Europe, the Allies were making great headway against the Axis. The Red Army was steadily pushing west, all but taking Romania and Hungary out of the war in the process. Meanwhile, Britain and America were getting ready to invade Europe head-on. The Allied commanders knew that invading Western Europe would be extremely difficult and would cost many lives, so they began planning in late 1943. They gave the invasion the codename of *Operation Neptune*; today more commonly known as *D-Day*. "D-Day" simply stands for "Day Day," which stood for the day the invasion took place, June 6, 1944.

The Allied commander decided that the French peninsula of *Normandy* was the best place to invade because it was only a short distance across the English Channel. It also had wide open beaches that could accommodate an invasion force of more than one million men.

Once the invasion took place, the Americans landed on beaches named Omaha and Utah, while the British landed at Sword and Gold beaches. Many Canadians were also involved in the invasion, landing at Juno beach.

The Germans were also ready with nearly 400,000 men and more than 2,000 tanks. Most of the Luftwaffe was fighting on the Eastern Front, but the Germans had plenty of anti-aircraft guns to counter the Allied fighters and bombers. The Germans also had time to erect plenty of defensive fortifications on and near the beaches. Barbwire greeted the Allied soldiers as they rushed from their transport boats to the beaches. On bluffs above the beaches, German soldiers sat in pillboxes and machine gun nests, waiting to shoot the advancing force.

Both sides suffered high casualties in the initial fighting, but after a couple of days the Germans had fallen back to more defensible locations away from the beaches. The German retreat allowed the Allies to keep landing troops and to advance into the French interior. By August 30, the Allies had liberated coastal France, giving them a decisive victory.

D-Day was the largest amphibious military invasion in history. Both sides suffered more than 200,000 casualties, which to the already retreating Germans was devastating.

Nearly 40,000 French civilians also died during the D-Day Invasion, making it one of the deadliest battles for civilians in human history.

OLD BLOOD AND GUTS

As General Eisenhower plotted the Allies' strategy from the war room, it was up to other generals to carry out the plans successfully on the battlefield. And there was no other general who was more respected by his troops, and his enemies for that matter, than American General George Patton, often referred to affectionately as "Old Blood and Guts."

Like most of the high-ranking American officers of his time, Patton went to the prestigious United States Military Academy at West Point, New York before embarking on a career in the military. Patton knew that tanks were the future of warfare, so when the United States entered World War I in 1917 he volunteered to lead a tank brigade.

After the war, Patton continued to train American soldiers in tank warfare and kept up on all the latest tank tactics coming out of Europe. When World War II began and the American high command saw how important tank warfare was in the war, Patton was promoted to general and given command of the 2nd Armored Division.

Patton became known as "Old Blood and Guts" when he led the 2nd Armored Division during Operation Torch, where he defeated the Desert Fox and the Afrika Korps.

General Patton was not afraid to state his opinion, even to his superiors, and often replaced his subordinates if he didn't think they were up to the task. Because of those personality traits, other officers often didn't like him, although to those that mattered, such as Eisenhower, they were willing to overlook his personality flaws.

The rank and file enlisted men all-respected Patton. He made regular inspections of the camps to make sure all his men were well-supplied and often visited the injured in the hospitals. When the battles started, he was always leading from the front.

After the Allied invasion of France, Patton was given command of the Third Army, where he successfully led his tanks into Germany at the end of the war.

Patton was assigned to an administrative post after the war where he was involved in a car accident on December 8, 1945. He died from his injuries on December 21, 1945 in a hospital in Heidelberg, Germany.

George Patton will forever be remembered as much for his flamboyant style and sometimes brash attitude as his battlefield victories. But there is no doubt that General George Patton was probably the best battlefield general in the Allied army.

DID YOU KNOW?

- The full name of the Japanese Zero was the Mitsubishi A6M Zero. If you think part of that name sounds familiar, it is probably the Mitsubishi part. The Mitsubishi corporation made the planes and it is the same Mitsubishi corporation that makes cars today.

- American pilots, sailors, and Marines referred to Zeros as "Zeke."

- The American 82nd Airborne Division formed on August 15, 1942. It was the first American airborne division, playing an important role in the invasion of Italy and the Normandy campaign.

- Because most of the battles in the Pacific were fought in either jungles or on small, rocky islands, or both, tanks were rarely used.

- The P-51 Mustang was the most effective American fighter plane during the war. It was used in both theaters and by the British as well as the Americans.

- Kamikaze pilots believed they were following the actions of the medieval Japanese warriors known as samurais, so they often carried samurai swords with them on their last mission.

THE WARSAW GHETTO UPRISING

After the Axis defeat at Stalingrad, things began to fall apart very quickly for Germany on the Eastern Front. The Hungarian and Romanian pro-Axis governments collapsed, and Finland was pushed back in the north by the Red Army. As the Germans retreated west, they initiated a *scorched earth policy.* A scorched earth policy is when an army destroys all infrastructure as it retreats, including highways, railroads, bridges, and telephone lines. The fighting on the Eastern Front was already particularly brutal, with both sides rarely taking POWs (prisoners of war), instead usually killing them and massacring civilians.

The German retreat was bad news for some people. Many of the *Baltic* peoples and *Ukrainians* sided with the Germans. It wasn't that they particularly liked the Germans or that they were Nazis, but more so that they hated being part of the Soviet Union.

Other people were more than happy to see the Germans retreat. Most Russians were glad to see them leave their country and Jews throughout Eastern Europe breathed a sigh of relief when they saw the Wehrmacht moving west.

But not everyone was willing to wait for the Red Army. Some people wanted to take up whatever arms they could and help the Red Army make the Wehrmacht retreat even faster. Armed citizen partisan groups formed throughout eastern Europe and Jews in the *ghettos* also began to rebel. Ghettos were neighborhoods of major cities where the Nazis forced the Jews to live.

On April 19, 1943, the residents of the Warsaw Jewish ghetto rebelled against the Nazis.

The Jewish rebels were organized and numbered about 1,000 fighters, but they were ill-equipped and no match for the better armed and trained Wehrmacht and SS members. The uprising lasted until May 16, 1943, before it was brutally suppressed by the Germans. It is estimated that more than 50,000 of the ghetto's residents were either killed during the uprising or executed in the days following. More than 30,000 surviving residents were then rounded up and shipped off to concentration camps, where many of them died.

Only seventeen Germans died and more than ninety were wounded in the fighting.

The Jewish Rebel survivors later said that they never expected to win the battle but standing up was what mattered.

GERMANY'S LAST GAMBLE IN THE WEST

After the successful D-Day invasion, things looked good for the Allies. The Allies marched through the streets of Paris, giving the city back to the French, who had lost the city and the country four years earlier. To many of the Allies, it seemed as though it would only be a matter of days before the Germans surrendered. After all, they were losing the few allies they had on the Eastern Front and it was only a matter of time until the Red Army was on Germany's border.

But Hitler and his commanders had one last trick up their sleeves.

They decided to transfer some of their elite *Waffen SS* units from the Eastern Front to France for a final counteroffensive in the west. They hoped that the counteroffensive would either buy them some extra time on the Eastern Front, allowing them to divert precious resources to fight the Soviets, or it could possibly give them leverage in peace negotiations with the Western Allies.

The Germans called the counteroffensive the *Ardennes Counteroffensive* because it began in the Ardennes Forest in northern France, but the Allies knew it as the *Battle of the Bulge*. It was called the Battle of the Bulge because the German forces pressed deep against the Allied forces, creating a "bulge" in the front line.

The Germans used the defensive fortifications they built in northern France, known as the *Siegfried Line,* to launch their lighting assault on December 16, 1944. The Germans hoped to push all the way to the coast, trapping Allied forces in a pocket in Belgium and the Netherlands. The early battle went well for the Germans. Heavy snow and cloudy skies limited the ability of the Allied air forces and the surprise attack almost did reach the coast.

But the Allies numerical superiority proved to be too much for the Germans. After intense fighting that left nearly 90,000 Allied forces killed or injured and nearly 100,000 German casualties, the Allies were victorious on January 25, 1945.

The number of men the Germans lost was devastating because they had no way of replacing them. All able-bodied men were expected to fight on the Eastern Front, so after the Battle of the Bulge there was no real resistance in the West. Not only that, but the Luftwaffe in the West was all but wiped out by early 1945.

RAISING THE FLAG ON IWO JIMA

In early 1945, the war was going well for the Allies. The Germans had been beaten back all the way to their original borders and in the Pacific the Americans had taken the last few islands before they reached Japan. With that said, neither the Germans nor the Japanese were giving up very easily. The leaders of both governments knew that they would probably face war crimes trials if they lost, so they pushed their armies to fight to the last man. There was just one last stop for the Americans in the Pacific—Iwo Jima.

In many ways Iwo Jima is an insignificant island. It only covers just over eight square miles, has no native population, and has no valuable resources. But it did serve as a protective outpost for the Japanese military during World War II because of its location in the Pacific and its geography. The highest point on Iwo Jima is **Mount Suribachi,** which towers far above the island. Mount Suribachi gave the Japanese a defensive advantage: they could shoot their artillery down on American Marines invading the island and then hide in its many caves once the Americans began to work up the mountain.

The Battle of Iwo Jima began with a naval and aerial bombardment for ten days, which was then followed by an American Marine amphibious invasion on February 19, 1945. Although the Americans were able to quickly land thousands of Marines on the island and had the Japanese outnumbered about five to one, the Japanese at Iwo Jima put up some of the toughest resistance in both theaters of the war.

Japanese soldiers laid booby traps for the Marines and built machine gun nests in caves and crags throughout the island.

Finally, on March 26, 1945, the Americans could claim victory. But it came at great cost. Nearly 7,000 Americans died taking Iwo Jima, and of the 20,000 plus Japanese who defended the island only 216 were taken alive! Even the Japanese commanders were either killed in battle or committed **seppuku,** or ritual suicide, instead of being taken alive.

When the battle was over, six American Marines—Rene Gagon, Ira Hayes, Harold Schultz, Michael Strank, Harlon Block, and Franklin Sousley—were photographed by Associated Press photographer Joe Rosenthal, hoisting the American flag atop Mount Suribachi. This photograph became world-famous and is still well-known—you've no doubt seen the picture yourself.

The victory opened the final route for the Americans to Japan and the photograph seemed to give Americans a renewed sense of hope and pride.

DID YOU KNOW?

- The flag the Marines raised at Iwo Jima only had 48 stars. That's because Alaska and Hawaii didn't become states until 1959.

- President Roosevelt died on April 15, 1945 during his third term as president. Vice President Harry Truman became president and led the United States until the end of the war.

- Rommel, the Desert Fox, became involved in a plot to kill Hitler in 1944. Once his involvement was discovered, he was forced to commit suicide by cyanide poisoning.

- The M3 Stuart Light Tank used by the Allies throughout the war was produced in the United States and named for Civil War Confederate General J.E.B. Stuart.

- The Siegfried Line was named after an ancient German mythological hero. According to the myth, Siegfried killed a dragon and bathed in its blood, which made his skin impenetrable. The Germans hoped that their defensive fortifications would also be impenetrable.

THE BATTLE OF BERLIN

The war in Europe was all but over by the spring of 1945. Entire units of the German forces in Western Europe were surrendering to the Allies, but the situation was quite different on the Eastern Front. Because the Germans carried out many massacres on the civilian population of the Soviet Union when they were winning the war and would also often kill Soviet POWs, the Red Army was returning the favor. Surrendering German soldiers were executed and once the Red Army made its way into German territory, they sexually assaulted, murdered, and robbed countless German citizens.

The German military was left with no other alternative but to fight to the end. They held out a faint hope that they could kill enough Red Army soldiers to force them to retreat and then completely surrender to the Americans and British.

General Zhukov and the Red Army descended on the German capital of Berlin with three army groups of 2.5 million men on April 16, 1945. American and British bombers gave the Soviets air support in what is now known as the Battle of Berlin.

The Germans had few fighting age men left in their military, so they enlisted young boys and old men to defend Berlin. Many of Germany's top generals fought their way out of Berlin and went west to surrender to the British or Americans, although many more decided to "go down with the ship."

Far below the streets of Berlin, just before the final battle began, Hitler and his closest friends and advisors waited for the inevitable in a *bunker*. A bunker is a structure, usually made of cement, which protects people from airplane bombings and artillery shelling. On April 10, 1945, Hitler killed himself with a single gunshot to his head. His longtime girlfriend, Eva Braun, used cyanide poisoning to kill herself along with Hitler. Hitler's surviving loyal followers then took the remains to the surface of the bunker where they were burned in order to prevent the Red Army from desecrating his body.

Still, after the Soviets won the Battle of Berlin, they took Hitler's remains and moved them several times to prevent them from becoming some sort of memorial.

The war in Europe was officially over on May 8 and celebrations soon followed on Allied countries known as *V-E Day*, or "Victory in Europe Day."

THE HOLOCAUST

World War II affected civilian populations more than any other war before it. The German and Soviet armies regularly carried out retributions and massacres against enemy civilian populations and it was part of the Nazi policy to view the Jews as enemies of the German state. Once the Nazis came to power, they wasted no time in persecuting the Jews.

The Nazis began by enacting the *Nuremberg Laws* on September 15, 1935. These laws made it illegal for Jews living in Germany to work in certain professions or to marry non-Jews. Jews were also required to wear a yellow *Star of David* patch on their clothing when in public to signify their background. Any Jews, as well as non-Jews, who protested Nazi policies in any way were sent to *concentration camps.* A concentration camp is a prison where a certain population—men, women, and children—are sent during a war. The first Nazi concentration camps were opened in 1933 in Germany, but as the war went on many were opened in Eastern Europe. Some of the most notorious concentration camps, such as *Auschwitz*, were located outside of Germany.

The Nazi persecution of Jews and their other enemies, which included communists, homosexuals, and *Roma/Gypsies*, continued throughout the war. But even before the war began, on November 9, 1938, Nazi street fighters known as *stormtroopers* went on a rampage throughout Germany, destroying Jewish businesses and synagogues. This night became known as *Kristallnacht,* or the "night of broken glass."

Many Jews did what they could after Kristallnacht to leave Germany for England, the United States, or Palestine, but those who didn't were captured and sent to concentration camps. The *Gestapo* acted as the Nazi government's secret police, spying on the people and arresting any possible enemies. Millions of people died in the concentration camps, which was a shocking sight for Allied soldiers to see when they liberated them.

Many of these camps still exist and today visitors can walk through the camps and museums to learn about how horrific World War II was for the civilians caught in the crossfire.

FAT MAN AND LITTLE BOY

After the Germans were finally defeated, the Allies were able to turn their complete attention to the Japanese. The Soviets were able to start moving the Red Army across Siberia and the British began sailing their navy through the Pacific. But the Japanese showed no signs of surrendering, so the Allied high command began drawing up an invasion plan of Japan they called *Operation Downfall*.

The plan called for an Allied amphibious invasion of Japan's southernmost island in 1946, but even if successful it could have potentially cost tens of thousands of American lives. When Truman became president, he decided to go in another direction.

American scientists had been working on developing an atomic bomb in what is known as the *Manhattan Project*. Manhattan Project scientists worked in labs across the United States, but when it finally came to test their results, they used an isolated area of the desert in New Mexico. The first successful atomic bomb was exploded on July 16, 1945 in what is known as the *Trinity Test*.

When President Truman was alerted that the bomb had been successfully tested, he gave the go ahead to use it on Japan.

The cities of Hiroshima and Nagasaki were picked as the targets because they were the primary bases of the Imperial Japanese Navy. The larger of the two bombs was nicknamed "Fat Man" due to its large, oval shape, and the smaller of the two was named "Little Boy."

On August 6, 1945, the B-29 bomber, *Bokscar*, dropped Little Boy on Nagasaki. The American B-29 bomber, *Enola Gay*, dropped Fat Man on Hiroshima on August 9, 1945. The two bombs leveled both cities and killed more than 250,000 military and civilians. The Japanese surrendered to the Allies on August 15, 1945 (August 14 U.S. time due to the international dateline). *V-J Day* ("Victory over Japan Day") celebrations broke out across the United States, Australia, and other major Asian cities, as the realization that the war was finally over.

Representatives of the Japanese government signed the official surrender on September 2, 1945 on the deck of the *USS Missouri* in Tokyo Bay.

A HARSH PEACE

Defeating the Japanese and Germans proved to be only another step towards peace. Most of Europe and large parts of Asia would have to be rebuilt and then there was the matter of what to do with the representatives of the losing governments. In the case of Germany, Hitler and most of his top men had taken their lives at the end of the war, but there were still quite a few Nazis alive. And in Japan, most of the government and many of the military leaders also made it to the end of the war.

Before the war was even over, the leaders of the major Allied nations decided at a conference in *Yalta*, Russia and then after the war in *Potsdam*, Germany, that Germany would be occupied militarily by the winners. It was decided that the leaders of the German military and the Nazi Party would be tried for *war crimes*. The trials were held in the German city of *Nuremberg*, which was chosen because it was the location where the Nazis held many of their public rallies after they came to power.

The *Nuremberg Trials* were held from November 20,1945 until October 1,1946. More than 200 people were tried, with most being convicted on a wide range of crimes. Some of the convicted, such as architect Albert Speer who received a twenty-year sentence, expressed repentance. But many of the Nazis, such as theorist Alfred Rosenberg, were defiant even after they were sentenced to hang in the gallows.

The Allied troops continued to occupy Germany and finally it was formally split into East and West Germany in 1949. This officially began the *Cold War*.

Meanwhile, in Japan a similar course of events unfolded.

The Americans occupied Japan as they did Germany and conducted war crimes trials, although they weren't as lengthy and didn't involve as many defendants as in Germany.

On April 29, 1946, the Allies tried twenty-eight high ranking Japanese officials in what is known as the *Tokyo Trial*. Former Prime Minister, Hideki Tojo, and six other men were sentenced to death. The executions were carried out at the Sugamo Prison on December 23, 1948.

After the harsh peace conditions were imposed on the former Axis nations, the United States then helped rebuild the countries. Europe especially needed help to restore its infrastructure, so the U.S. government initiated the *Marshall Plan* in 1948. The Marshall Plan set aside about $17 billion in grants for Europe, which were dispersed from 1948 to 1951.

It would take many years, but by the mid-1950s, Western Europe was back up and running. Eastern Europe, however, was under the control of the Soviet Union. But that's another book!

AN IRON CURTAIN OVER EUROPE

When the war in Europe was over, most of the survivors were ready to rebuild their communities and countries. They didn't really care about politics too much and just wanted to get back to normal. But almost as soon as everything was over, it became clear to most that Europe would never be normal again. In every country that the Red Army occupied in Eastern Europe, Stalin made sure that communist *puppet governments* were installed. A puppet government is a government that is heavily influenced or even controlled by a foreign government. In this case, the countries of Poland, Hungary, Czechoslovakia, and Bulgaria pretty much took their orders from Moscow.

And Stalin was able to successfully rebuild the Soviet Union by reincorporating all the smaller countries that were part of it before the war.

Finally, the Soviets got half of Germany and half of the city of Berlin. However, they still wanted more. When the Western leaders refused to give Berlin to Stalin, he surrounded the city with troops and cut off West Berlin's access to the outside world. The West responded by flying supplies to West Berlin nonstop, from June 1948 to May 1949, in what became known as the *Berlin Airlift*.

It was clear to most leaders in the West that, although Stalin may have been their ally in World War II, he was now their enemy. Winston Churchill declared in a 1946 speech at Westminster College in Fulton, Missouri that "an *iron curtain* has descended across the Continent." The continent he was talking about was Europe and the iron curtain was communism.

The world quickly became divided between the United States and its allies, and the Soviet Union and its allies in what became known as the *Cold War*. It was referred to as a "Cold War" because the two major nations never fought each other directly, although there were several related, smaller wars and battles throughout the world until 1991.

After Stalin backed down and allowed access to West Berlin, a flood of people from East Berlin and East Germany came into West Germany. Stalin's successor, Nikita Khrushchev, ordered all the communist nations of Eastern Europe to close their borders. As a result, the communist government of East Germany erected the *Berlin Wall* on August 13, 1961. Much of the wall was made of concrete, with barbed wire also used in certain places. Hundreds of people died trying to cross over the wall until it was dismantled on November 9, 1989.

THIRD QUIZ TIME!

1. What was the name of the Pacific island where the victorious American Marines famously raised the American flag?

   a. Iwo Jima
   b. Hawaii
   c. Sicily

2. Fat Man and _____ were the nickname of the atomic bombs dropped on Japan.

   a. Frosty
   b. Billy
   c. Little Boy

3. Germany's last major offensive in the West was called?

   a. Hitler's Gamble
   b. The Battle of the Bulge
   c. The Battle of Belgium

4. "V-E" stands for?

   a. Victory over Europe Day
   b. Victory over Japan Day
   c. Victory over Everyone Day

5. In what year did World War II end?

   a. 1945
   b. 1939

INTERESTING QUOTES

The Red Army and Navy and the whole Soviet people must fight for every inch of Soviet soil, fight to the last drop of blood for our towns and villages...onward, to victory!

Josef Stalin – July 1941

Boys, if you ever pray, pray for me now.

Harry S. Truman – April 1945

Attacks on cities are strategically justified in so far as they tend to shorten the war and so preserve the lives of allied soldiers.

Arthur "Bomber" Harris – March 1945

QUIZ ANSWERS

Answers: First Quiz Time!

1. c - Versailles Treaty

2. b - Adolf Hitler

3. a - Axis Powers

4. a - Munich Agreement

5. b - Reich

Answers: Second Quiz Time!

1. Poland

2. December 7, 1941

3. The Soviet Union

4. They went through the Low Countries instead

5. The Balkans or Balkan Peninsula

6. Italy, Japan, Hungary, Bulgaria, Romania, or Finland

Answers: Third Quiz Time!

1. a - Iwo Jima

2. c - Little Boy

3. b - The Battle of the Bulge

4. a - Victory over Europe Day

5. a - 1945

CONCLUSION

World War II was certainly devastating and had a huge impact on those involved, with its effects felt all over the world and even still today. Perhaps the greatest impact that World War II had on the world was how it changed *geopolitics*. Geopolitics describes the political relations between the world's nations.

Gone was the old colonial system that Great Britain and France dominated. Those countries were unable to keep most of their colonies, so those colonies became independent countries. France and Britain still had a lot of influence in the world, but the two most powerful countries became the United States and the Soviet Union.

The Americans and Soviets became engaged in a struggle against each other known as the Cold War. Both sides struggled to influence smaller countries and push their view of government, economics, and politics on the world. The Cold War may have officially ended in the early 1990s, but it continues today in many ways.

World War II also introduced many words, phrases, and concepts into the American vocabulary. Words like "genocide" and "concentration camp" unfortunately became more common as a result of World War II, and after the atomic bombs were dropped on Japan so did the word "atomic." In fact, the 1950s was often said to be the "Atomic Age."

The 1950s was also the "Space Age," as it marked the beginning of space exploration, which was spurned by World War II rocket technology. German scientists, such as Werner von Braun, helped establish NASA and the American space program, which in the 1950s and 1960s seemed to indicate that there was no limit to American achievement.

World War II also helped end the Great Depression and sent the United States into an economic boom. When American soldiers, sailors, and marines came home after World War II, they were able to buy new homes and flash cars. They also wasted no time in starting a family and became known as the "Baby Boomers," the most populous generation in American history.

World War II had a massive effect on both people and places around the world. No matter where you are, if you look around enough, you will no doubt see some of those impacts even today.